This little book was written by
my mother Mrs Shelland Smith

To Evelyn Bash with regards

from

Tina Lever Howley

45.-

POEMS AND PAINTINGS

POEMS AND PAINTINGS

BY GEORGINE SHILLARD

M · C · M · L · I · I · I

This book has been printed by The Ram Press, New York
in the summer of 1953.

CONTENTS

FOREWORD   5

HIGHLIGHTS FROM THE LIFE OF GEORGINE SHILLARD   7

THE FLORIDA GULF COAST ART CENTER   17

AN APPRECIATION   20

POEMS

ECSTASY   23

"IN NOBIS REGNAT ILLE"   25

SPRING SONG   26

RAINY DAY   28

ALWAYS A CHILD   29

TO THE DELAWARE   31

THE GREAT OLD LINDEN TREE   32

AN ATOM OF ETERNITY   33

GENTLY, YE STRONG!   34

STAR LOVE   35

THE CALL   36

WHO HAS NOT DREAMED OF BEAUTY   37

NATURE   38

THE OAK TREE   39

CHURCH WINDOW   40

BLITHE BIRD   41

THE ROSE   42

PEACE OF MY CHILDHOOD   43

SHIRKING   44

PAINTINGS

GAY NINETIES

AT THE FEET OF THE MASTER

YOUTH EMBARKING ON THE BOAT OF LIFE

EARLY STUDY
   PAINTED IN CECILIA BEAUX' STUDIO
   AT THE PENNSYLVANIA ACADEMY OF FINE ARTS

END OF THE ROAD, SEA ISLAND, GEORGIA

ANNE HEEBNER ON PORCH AT BOOTHBAY HARBOR

HIGH BUTTON BOOTS

BALLOON WOMAN, PARIS

MARKET WOMAN, GUERNSEY, CHANNEL ISLANDS

TAOS, NEW MEXICO

LOCK, NEW HOPE, PENNSYLVANIA

TAOS, NEW MEXICO

FOREWORD

The culmination of an idea which follows a long life of service and during which time the vision has moments of frustration, periods of inward expansion and many hours of fear and hope for its ultimate fruition, sometimes is evidenced in a final goal of triumph.

This little book is the humble expression of just such an unfoldment of an early ambition. It is the torch of faith in its fulfillment. It is one small phase of a great program that in spiritual and material form seeks to find expression.

A few years ago I met the author in New York City and for perhaps an hour or more she told me about her hopes and plans for an institution which might teach the spiritual and the human values of life thru the Arts. American citizenship, moral integrity and creative enlightenment all had opportunity for development in the underlying theme of her idea. The time, the place and the world situation gave emphasis to the sore need for youth-education thru such a basic conception of growth and human progress by means of Art in its many ramifications.

Here in the mercenary hustle and bustle of a great city came to light a spark of extraordinary significance couched in terms of practical attainment. The messages within these poems were bearing the fruit of profound and studied thought in their final manifestation.

Age had not quenched the vision, merely tempered it to meet civilization's needs. The early voice of an inspired moment, nurtured of itself in poetic, visual and spiritual expression grew stronger with the years. And now that early dream, budding into blossom, emerges to full flower.

In sensitive verse, in colorful pigment and in architectural form the author has brought forth the oneness of her conception, now to be extended and enriched in sunny Florida for all who seek to find, and for all who find, a fuller life and a closer walk with God.

"Out of the Oneness it came,
   a live note from far off within me.
I knew it as of the true,
   all-perfect, enduring, immortal,
I felt it of me, but it came from the life of all ages
From earth, sky and air, nothing dead, but all living."

G. S.

ROYAL BAILEY FARNUM

Hampton, Connecticut
May 10, 1953

6

HIGHLIGHTS FROM THE LIFE
OF GEORGINE SHILLARD

Georgine Shillard* chose a site on a bluff at Clearwater, Florida, for her house, the Georgine Shillard Gallery and the Florida Gulf Coast Art Center, because it reminded her of the bluff overlooking the Delaware at Edgewater Park, New Jersey where, as she grew up, she played with fairies, learned to meditate, sat with her beaux and wrote "To the Delaware," her first poem.

She was born Georgine Northrop Wetherill, the eldest of five children, quiet, thoughtful, and so in love with the natural world that she can still remember going to sleep hugging the stars. Her earliest companions were Arathusa, an imaginary sprite who responded to her every wish, whether she wanted to run with the wind or sit and watch sunlight dance on the water, and her equally responsive grandfather Northrop.

Her grandfather tried to resist her only once. He hedged when she demanded to go with him to Atlantic City, where he always stayed alone until the end of the hay fever season, by promising to take her when she had learned to dress herself. But when she enquired, gazing earnestly up at him, "Grandfather, how can I do myself up behind when I'm in front?", the Philadelphia lawyer succumbed. He took her to Atlantic City. The

7

* Mrs. C. Shillard Smith.

wife of the proprietor of the United States hotel did her
up behind, and his friends and fellow jurists, Garrison,
McMurtrie, McVey and McAllister helped entertain
her. She was four.

The following winter she started school, riding to St.
Mary's Hall snuggled under a buffalo robe in the sleigh.

At six she began attending the Farnum School, always
walking as far as the post office with Mr. Shipman, who
lived a little farther along the Delaware bluff. Mr. Paul
Shipman was considered odd because he continued in
retirement his newspaperman's habit of dining at four
o'clock in the morning, but his fascination for Georgine
Wetherill was entirely literary.

Their friendship grew until she was only too eager to
row one of his visitors clear across the Delaware and up
Neshaminy Creek to catch his train. It was a two-mile
row, but after all, wasn't she rowing Mr. Prentice, the
editor of the Louisville Journal?

After graduation from Farnum, she journeyed daily to
the Case & Hallowell School in Philadelphia, first seeing
that the younger children, Sara, Christine, Price and
Isabel were dressed, and helping Katharine, the maid, to
fill all the oil lamps.

In the horse car she sat with bent head, gazing down
at her feet in the straw. Aware of her fellow passengers,
effected by their thoughts, she seldom raised her eyes,
except to glance shyly at Walt Whitman, who used to
sit by the driver wrapped in a great cloak, his white beard
riffling in the breeze.

How she longed to meet him, and how she begged her
mother to let her go to Boston with her governness, Miss

8

Caroline Lorenz, who knew Lowell, Mark Twain and Holmes! She read them all. Far into the night, long after her mother had carried her bedroom lamp away, she huddled at the top of the stairs, turning her book this way and that to catch the dim hall light.

She had a gift for languages, and was a favorite of her Latin teacher, Miss Case. "Georgine Wetherill," Miss Case remarked to a friend, "does something for me the moment she enters a room."

But her grandfather was appalled when she told him she'd like to study Greek. "My darling," he said, kissing her hand, "women are made to be adored."

And her mother, anxious because she had experienced a momentary blindness on her way home from school with Sara one day, sent her to Europe with her Aunt Kay, who was taking the Rosengarten girls.

She returned from Europe merrily engaged to three young men. They all came calling at Edgewater Park, and one even dared the informality of calling her on the telephone, a contraption which had just been installed. "Young whippersnapper," her grandfather growled.

While she was still trying to decide which to marry, a cousin, Katy Brown, came to visit from Boston, and Georgine bet Sara she could get Katy a beau for the university ball. She did, too. At a dinner party she met Charles Shillard Smith, a man of the world and an accomplished flirt, and she charmed him into going to the ball and being delightful to Katy.

It was raining when Mr. Wetherill came to fetch the girls home from the party. Charles Shillard Smith put them into the carriage and then stood in the rain as they drove off, still holding Mr. Wetherill's big umbrella.

The next afternoon he returned the umbrella with a book for Georgine.

They were married in the spring.

Georgine Shillard and her husband went to Philadelphia every morning; he to his office and she to the Academy of Fine Arts, where she studied first with Henri, then with Cecilia Beau, Breckenridge, Carter and Henry Thouron.

When she entered sketches in a competition for a scholarship to Paris, it was Thouron who said, "If you won, you'd give it to so-and-so, wouldn't you? He's hungry." Whereupon she withdrew from the competition and vowed never to enter another.

However, she did go abroad upon the advice of her doctor after a severe illness, taking just six hundred dollars which had to last until her return. Two men, a stranger and Whistler, made her stay in Europe momentous.

She met the stranger in London. He spoke in the Vegetarian Restaurant in the Tottenham Court Road, and when he finished, Georgine Shillard thanked him. She has never forgotten his long, searching look or her own clear conviction that he *knew* something. All he said to her was, "Go to Tavistock Square and attend a meeting of the Theosophical Society.

In Paris, after having criticisms from Simon and Cortet, who told her that her academy had taught her nothing, she decided to study at Whistler's school in the

Rue du Bac with her friend, Anne Heebner, her Uncle Elisha Kent Kane Wetherill and his friend, Richard Blossom Farley.

They were delighted. "Whistler'll say, 'Here's another one of those clever Academy students,'" her uncle chuckled.

But Whistler was ill, and Mrs. Clifford Adams, the only one of his students he ever authorized to teach, taught her to set up and use Whistler's palette.

Three Whistler precepts also became Georgine Shillard's: first, to draw the model for a week; second, to establish the value of the background; and third, to take a deep breath and paint on the breath.

Because Whistler forbade mixed classes, Georgine Shillard and Anne Heebner went to one class, Elisha Wetherill and Richard Farley to another. But they discussed Whistler whenever they met, and especially on Sunday evenings when they gathered at the modest pension where the girls lived within walking distance of the studio.

Elisha Kent Kane Wetherill, who was to become a National Academician, used to marvel at Whistler's subtleties, "Why," he'd say, "Whistler can point out as many as fourteen tones in a face, from eye to nose and back again, all so subtly blended that they can hardly be detected." And he'd consume quantities of the crackers and caviar his niece always provided, because she knew he spent too much of his small income for books and picture frames and too little for food.

Then, late in the evening, replete with Whistler and caviar, he, Farley, Anne Heebner and any other friends who had dropped in used to settle back to listen while

Georgine Shillard read Emerson aloud.

Georgine Shillard's knowledge and acceptance of the teachings of Theosophy were instinctive from her earliest childhood. As a small child with an uncommonly keen awareness of the natural world, she played with elves and fairies. When she was a mere girl, meditating at sunset by the Delaware, she learned her oneness with the world.

And so, she naturally became an enthusiastic member of the Theosophic Society as soon as she attended her first meeting in London's Tavistock Square. Naturally, too, she studied the Veda, Upanishads and Bhagavad-Gita avidly. And, after her return to Philadelphia she became very active in the work of the Society.

For thirteen years she inserted a weekly advertisement in Philadelphia newspapers, headed "Everyday problems solved in the light of Theosophy," and spent several hours each Wednesday at the rooms of the Society, advising all who answered it. There was no fee, no obligation, and so all sorts of people brought their troubles and their fears.

A worried young university student, whose parents had told him he was going to hell for attending university dances, left confident and happy after being told that dancing was at the beginning of all religion and that "it was the love of God and their fellow men that prompted people to dance."

Angry and unhappy women came. One who threatened to take from her husband "every cent he has," because of some real or imagined unfaithfulness, left the Society's rooms humbly begging forgiveness for her own

GEORGINE SHILLARD, ART STUDENT

photo: Trude Fleischmann

GEORGINE SHILLARD — 1953

bad nature.

"Men's troubles usually arise within themselves," Georgine Shillard says, reminiscing about those Wednesdays.

She went to India, to Adyar, where Theosophists from every part of the world gathered for the Society's jubilee. With what pleasure she remembers hearing great Theosophists lecture beneath the huge banyan tree! With what gratitude she recalls the morning prayers of Buddists, Mohammedans, Jains, Christians, and the saying of Annie Besant that united them all—"Oh, hidden life, vibrant in every atom; Oh, hidden light, shining in every creature; Oh, hidden love, embracing all in oneness! May each who feels himself as one with Thee, know he is also one with every other."

In London she met Krishnamurti, whom she reveres, and whose book, "Let Understanding Be the Law," became her bible.

Theosophy helped crystallize Georgine Shillard's great longing to help humanity into a desire to bring about a closer understanding between peoples of all races and all religions by means of a universal language —art.

For decades she held fast to her dream of a school devoted to all arts and available to all people, and at last she was able to make her dream come true by founding and supporting the Gulf Coast Art Center.

"From the beginning, Tina shared my dream," she says of her daughter, who, having inherited the Wetherill talent for art, is now the world-famous designer, Tina Leser.

She smiles, thinking aloud about her daughter. "Tina has a talent for music, too. And how she loves animals! We first learned of this love by giving her some ducklings for Easter when she was four. She'd sit happily on a step while the ducklings crowded under her skirts, and how we'd laugh to see them peep out and then draw back again."

"Tina introduced the architects, Nitzchke and Parker, whom I chose to design the first Art Center building," her mother recalls. "And I was very pleased when she decided to use her talents and her practical knowledge for the benefit of the students by establishing the Tina Leser Workshop. Profits from the workshop go to the students and the Center; my daughter takes nothing."

Dr. Royal Bailey Farnum of the Rhode Island School of Design was the first outside her family with whom Georgine Shillard shared her dream of the Art Center. In gratitude for his encouragement and advice, she asked him to write the foreword for this book.

The people of Clearwater helped by raising funds to build the Ceramic Building for which Miss Mary E. Johnston of Cincinnati and Clearwater contributed the kilns. The Disston Tool Company gave hand tools for the woodworking shop, and Mr. R. M. Thompson, Jr., a Clearwater contractor, contributed the clearing and surfacing of the parking lot. Mr. and Mrs. Arthur E. Yahn, who gave the entrance gates, are among others who have made greatly appreciated gifts to the Art Center. And more than five hundred current members of the Florida Gulf Coast Art Center together contribute several thousand dollars annually to its support.

All the rest—the *vision*, land, buildings, equipment,

and the sizeable remainder of the running expenses—is the gift of Georgine Shillard, who is convinced that she was instructed by a Master and guided by her star. As following pages show, the gift is priceless.

Lorna K. Tuck

Georgine Shillard delights to share the chart reproduced on the opposite page with all Theosophists. It recalls a moment of illumination in her own life. The moment was sunrise; the place a lichened rock near Christine's Tower on the coast of Maine. She had gone out to lie on the rock one evening after receiving an intense emotional shock, and had fallen asleep there. As the sun rose in the early morning she awakened gradually, feeling life rise in her body from the elemental stone through the various elemental kingdoms to the supreme consciousness of her solar self. Her misery was gone. Comforted to be part of the whole, she dedicated herself to the service of humanity. The Gulf Coast Art Center is an expression of that service.

On the morning of May 6, 1953 Georgine Shillard found on her desk this chart, drawn on the back of the professional letterhead of John A. Herring, M.D. Roentgenologist, St. Petersburg, Fla. Neither she nor any of her household had ever seen it before.

A call was put through to St. Petersburg, and Mrs. Herring, who answered, explained that Dr. Herring had been dead ten years, and that the chart, which she herself had never seen, had probably been made by her husband about fifteen years earlier, when he was giving radio talks at Clearwater on various subjects for the layman.

Dr. Herring, who had previously taught anatomy at Cornell and Ann Arbor, practiced in Florida from 1925 until his death in November 1943. The chart is reproduced with Mrs. Herring's permission.

MANIFESTATIONS
OF
LIFE

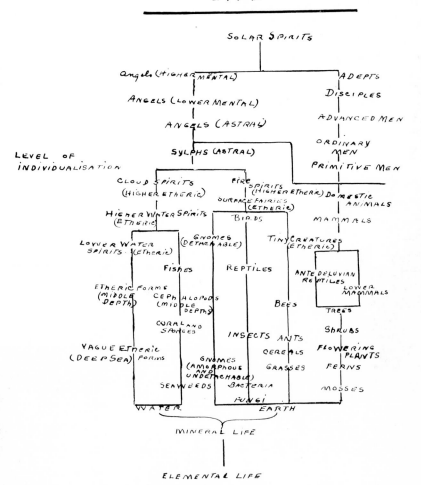

SOLAR SPIRITS

Angels (HIGHER MENTAL)   ADEPTS

                                                         DISCIPLES

Angels (LOWER MENTAL)

                                                    ADVANCED MEN

          ANGELS (ASTRAL)

                                                         ORDINARY
                                                            MEN
          SYLPHS (ASTRAL)

LEVEL OF   PRIMITIVE MEN
INDIVIDUALISATION

   CLOUD SPIRITS   FIRE SPIRITS
   (HIGHER ETHERIC)   (HIGHER ETHERIC) Domestic
                     SURFACE FAIRIES   ANIMALS
                        (ETHERIC)
   HIGHER WATER SPIRITS   BIRDS   MAMMALS
   (ETHERIC)
                      GNOMES   TINY CREATURES
                   (DETACHABLE)   (ETHERIC)
   LOWER WATER
   SPIRITS (ETHERIC)
          FISHES   REPTILES   ANTEDELUVIAN
                                     REPTILES
                                               LOWER
   ETHERIC FORMS   MAMMALS
   (MIDDLE   CEPHALOPODS
    DEPTH)   (MIDDLE   BEES   TREES
               DEPTH)
          CORAL AND
          SPONGES   SHRUBS

   VAGUE ETHERIC   INSECTS ANTS   FLOWERING
   (DEEP SEA) FORMS   PLANTS
                         GNOMES   CEREALS FERNS
                        (AMORPHOUS
                           AND
                      UNDETACHABLE) GRASSES
          SEAWEEDS   BACTERIA   MOSSES
                         FUNGI
     WATER   EARTH

          MINERAL LIFE

          ELEMENTAL LIFE

The Main Gallery, erected by Georgine Shillard, provides about four thousand square feet of exhibition space and houses several small studios and workshops. *Contemporary Painting*, one of the South's foremost exhibitions of modern art, originates here.

The entrance gates are the gift of Mr. and Mrs. Arthur E. Yahn.

THE FLORIDA GULF COAST ART CENTER
A DREAM COME TRUE

Georgine Shillard's crowning achievement is the Florida Gulf Coast Art Center, incorporated as a non-profit educational foundation dedicated to public service, and housed in four contemporary buildings in spacious grounds adjoining those of her own home and gallery at Belleair, Clearwater, Florida.

She dreamed of a school which would aim to help students, both old and young, attain reverent understanding of life and their part in it through the medium of all the arts. And after decades of planning, she made the dream come true by giving more than $275,000 in land, buildings, equipment and cash, by arousing the interest of the community, and by seeking out the zealous director, Harry W. Brown and such inspired teachers as William Pachner, Doris Lee, Ken J. Uyemura, Arnold Blanch, Gabor Peterdi, Tina Leser, Mary S. Clay and Robert Spencer Carr.

And Georgine Shillard gave the ownership and control of the Art Center to the community legally by deeding the land, buildings and equipment to an organization of its citizens known as the Florida Gulf Coast Art Center, Inc.

Painters, ceramists, designers, writers, weavers and woodcraftsmen work together at the Florida Gulf Coast Art Center in the atmosphere of "enlightened understanding and fellowship" conceived by the founder.

All are welcome, from the totally untaught to advanced students, and evening classes are offered especially for those interested in art as an avocation.

On Saturdays hundreds of children, who receive free instruction and free supplies, throng the campus.

Every Tuesday evening members and guests gather to open national, state or local exhibitions, to hear distinguished foreigners and professional artists, to see art films, or to enjoy programs concerning architecture, religious art, literature, photography, interior decoration, ceramics.

All nations, races and religions are equally respected at the Art Center. The founder is especially pleased by the recent registration of Japanese students, because her ultimate aim has been eventually to further understanding between men and nations through the medium of the universal language of art.

In the Tina Leser Workshop at the Gulf Coast Art Center, students learn basic design and processes of screen-making for printing materials, wallpapers, greeting cards and many other articles. They sell their designs to manufacturers through the Tina Leser Workshop Studio in New York, and receive two-thirds of the proceeds. The other third helps support the Art Center's Fine Arts program.

The Art Center's Christmas bazaar sells students' paintings, etchings, engravings, ceramics, wood sculpture, hand-weaving and greeting cards, and its literary agency markets manuscripts written by students and graduates of the creative writing course.

In every possible way the Florida Gulf Coast Art Center brings the aesthetic values of the Fine Arts into the life of the community. And, although it has been

The entrance facade of the Library Building, with the entrance to the Main Gallery in the distance. The Library Building, which is also the gift of Georgine Shillard, contains three thousand square feet used for exhibitions, meetings and study groups.

below:
Contributions from the people of Clearwater built the Ceramics Building in the foreground. Georgine Shillard gave the Wood-working Building in the background, and equipped it with thousands of dollars worth of the finest wood-working machinery. Hand tools were given by the Disston Tool Company.

Children look forward eagerly to Saturday classes at the Florida Gulf Coast Art Center, where they may have free instruction in painting, drawing, ceramics and woodworking. The Art Center supplies them with easels, paints, brushes, paper and clay. Hundreds come and have a wonderful time.

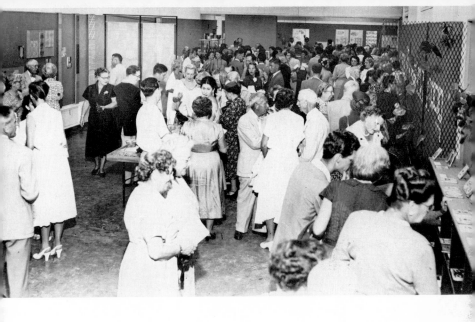

above:
Opening an exhibition at the
Florida Gulf Coast Art Center.

below:
Art Center demonstrations
are always popular.

photo: Trude Fleischman

Georgine Shillard's daughter, Tina Leser, world-famous designer of fabrics and fashions, in the Workshop at the Gulf Coast Art Center, which she instituted at her own expense.

operating only since 1949, it has already become what the founder meant it to be, "a focal point for all who labor to further human understanding through any of the fine arts."

"And now," Georgine Shillard entreats, "the vision is a reality and its usefulness to the community is proven. I have given all and more of my substance than I can afford, and I appeal to other benefactors to use the Art Center as a medium for helping others."

AN APPRECIATION

That a woman so eminent in affairs as Mrs. C. Shillard Smith should publish poems that stress what writers of mysticism have referred to as the "ghostly" aspect of life . . . the essence behind appearances . . . will give many people deep cause for thought. Mrs. Smith's poems share with her paintings, of which several are reproduced in this book, a concern with the inner life that only a few of her friends know she possesses.

Poets are sometimes accused of getting involved in philosophy to the exclusion of poetry. But Mrs. Smith's philosophy, so far from the homiletic-dialectic school, should speak to a large audience. Her circle of friends will cherish especially these expressions of her deepest insight.

It is with the greatest delight that I, as a poet, welcome this collection by Mrs. Smith, which gives voice to my own credo; namely, joy in life for life's own sake.

Norma Lay

POEMS

Out of the Oneness it came,
    a live note from far off within me.
I knew it as of the true,
    all-perfect, enduring, immortal.
I felt it of me,
    but it came from the Life of all ages,
From earth, sky and air,
    nothing dead, but all living,
Nothing written in small,
    but everywhere Spirit and Godhead,
As if the vast thought of the world
    and the tuneful eternal
Gave of its musical glory
    for one hallowed moment,
Gave of its oneness
    with power and perfect omniscience
Till the eyes that were sightless before
    saw what was hidden,
And mind that had labored before
    knew without thinking,
While the life of the whole and a part
    beat as one measure.

Prophets and mystics of old,
    whether Paynim or Christian,
Heard this same voice of the soul
    through all ages resounding.
Whether in pensive Ind or exalted Judea,
In Athens or Egypt

or here in the tumult and struggle,
Wherever aspiring has been,
    the voice of the Godhead has answered
And Man's feeble hands have gone fumbling
To catch and make lasting the Vision,
And Man's feeble mind has toiled nobly
    to grasp Truth completely
While sad, human hearts have born mutely
    their burden of ignorant living,
And laid it before the Power,
The first Poet
    who dreamed the beginning.

"IN NOBIS REGNAT ILLE"
(God Reigns in Us)

Some impulse eloquent of God spoke.
From inarticulate silence life awoke
And said, "Illumined soul! Let down
The floodgate of the years
And from the sea of passion, long suppressed,
Sing the glad song I gave you for the world,
For time has stilled the turmoil, and the winds
No longer storm. What need now to delay
The message eons taught you? Sing, I say,
      'In Nobis Regnat Ille'

"Through suffering and dumb pain, awake,
Arise and soar into the vast
With inward turning eyes that can direct
Thy eery flight out of the quickening sorrow of
                             your night
Back to the heart of God that is your home.

"What time I called you to the world of men
To cabin you in passion, and through pain
To lesson you anew in love and kindliness,
That your self-will should learn to listen true
And love the Law. Law is the song of life,
The lilt and measure for this little sphere.
We cannot rend, but child, we may transcend.
This the sole knowledge I give, and bid you live
And hold, and ne'er betray.
      In Nobis Regnat Ille."

What is it I sing
While the glad birds swing
'Midst the tender blossoms
Of budding spring?

Oh! rapturous part
Of their joyous art
In pulsing thicket
And flower and tree.

On hillside and mountain
And sunlit lea
All earth and sky
One ecstasy!

Forgot is the fold
Of the winter cold
Keeping them close
In her hoary fold.

Make way; give room
For joyous life,
Field and meadow and murmuring stream
Marshy fallow, the woods between

Throbbing all, in one blissful dream
Thrilling in praise
Of the glad, spring days
Showing live joy in such various ways.

Voicing sweet love.
Ours, let us prove—
Closer! closer! thy lips to mine,
How mad the world in the young springtime.

What is it I sing?
I scarcely know.
I love you; Oh
And I love Life so!

Close, heavy, sensuous day, too sweet, too full
On nature's languor. One can scarce take breath
For the moist odorous wantonness of earth,
Warm, motionless, the auburn-veilèd sun
Withholds her vital hording of the sea,
Rivers and lakes and fountains hidden deep
In mystery of some shadowy wilderness,
While earth lies silent in supreme suspense.
Empassioned, thrilled, for all the joys to be,
Clouds of fulfillment hang o'er field
Of latent fruitfulness; and the still air
Lingers expectant now of the near rain.

Always a child, and do you reproach me with this?
I do not grow like the world, well, what is amiss?
Is such happiness pictured there in the faces you
                                                    meet
Wan, anxious, hurrying phantoms of the streets
Dull, with desire of gold, ambitious of fame
Struggling just to exist . . . what is the bane,
What poisonous plant, corrupting my content
Would you prescribe?

And are you bent
On crushing all the natural force within
To prove in me how beauty's spoiled by sin?
For I do hold it as a crime indeed
To grope about blind, by the body's need
In darkness and distress, when burning bright
There is within the soul such glorious light
Such knowledge, all instinctive. I contend
It useless sacrifice, that will not mend
Materially, and Life itself depend   on some such course,
Like flower or tree
That cannot find the where-with-all to be
In the poor ground, dies there full patiently,
So, under the glad sky, even so would I.

But man is not so circumscribed by fate.
He can of his own character create
Surroundings suitable, if he but know,
Accept and cherish, come what will, or go,

The soul of him. And mine is a child's soul.
How can I plead a pardon for the goal
I aim at . . . only to feel with the world,
While slowly within the thought is unfurled
That the Maker intended. Strange, should the
                                    banner prove
Of little worth, woven by His discerning love
Here on this warp and woof of me
Here in this dedicated heart of me.

TO THE DELAWARE

(Jan. 18, 1893)

No sound disturbs the stillness of the air,
Thy living waters sleep, fair Delaware.
The sun ere now
Is set; with soft caress
Its last rays linger lovingly to press
Thy placid brow.
So still it is the silence seems to speak.

In childhood's hour I oft communed with thee.
Thy solemn silence spoke in sympathy
Whate'er the thought.
O now attune this heart,
And, as of old, thy beauteous thoughts impart.
They are still sought
And Life can fold no veil about my soul.

Yes, when no longer man shall think of me,
When this soul wanders through eternity,
Thou shalt still flow
And my soul still possess
Thy peace, and poise upon the wing
To bless
Thy murmurs low,
Those tender whisperings that awoke
Its sleep.

Do you hear the glad birds singing
In the great old linden tree?
Their little hearts rejoicing, gladsome
Just to be, only to be?

Do you see the children romping
Underneath the great old tree?
They can't keep still a moment
They're so happy just to be.

Dull heart, through living grown somber,
Go out 'neath the great old tree,
Rest, attune thyself to living
And once more rejoice to be.

O Life, what workest thou
With this poor soul of mine?
Thou seemeth not to know
It is a thought divine
And should not suffer so.

It had such faith in thee,
Trusted so utterly.
O dost thou truly think
Thou canst destroy it quite,
That fearful it will sink
And lose its little might
In struggling with thee?
Thou art deceived.
It has and ever holds
Its atom of eternity.

Yet Life, what workest thou
With this poor soul of mine?
Thou seemest not to know
It is a thought divine
And should not suffer so.

Gently through the world
Where human hearts are thirled
By thoughtless words,
Where toiling human herds
Plod drearily along,
Gently, ye strong!

The face that smiles in thine
Is mask of . . . ? Who can tell
What tragedy supine
What glimpse of hell
Its deeper self may plumb,
All mutely dumb?
Ye may not know.
Pass, gently go!

Wide, grim calamity
Can seldom be
Sole cause of misery,
But little things
Grate, discord gnawing deep,
Till the worn strings
Snap human souls
In useless bickerings.

Then, gently go,
For one can never know.

Alone,
Oh, all the awful anguish of our isolation.
Each one alone, his dark unfathomed night
Forever at his feet,
Part of unknown circle, each of us back stretching.
Into darkness lies our past
And out of that same void looms up our future.
We feel it now out in the night beneath the stars
That mock our love by their infinity
And make our vows light murmurs lost in space
No more momentous than this moony breeze.
Methinks a chillness shudders in the pale blue beams
And makes stars only real.

THE CALL

(April 1953)
Dedicated to President Eisenhower

Again and yet again the call
Goes forth.
"Man's need is great,"
The Master said,
"Who volunteers?"
Rally and inspire the nations.
Allay their fears.
Resolve to stand together
Against evil forces.
The great testing time
Is now.
Who has the vision?
Who volunteers?

WHO HAS NOT DREAMED OF BEAUTY!

Who has not dreamed of Beauty! But the dream
Is idle unless a skillful hand can shape
And out of dream-stuff make the thing to seem
More potent than the real itself has been,
For dreams are founded on the things that are.
O kindly force, lend thy mysterious power,
That with variety as nature's own
I may give birth to dreams that life has shown
More real than circumstance.

The hills fade mist-intoned in somber gray,
Save where the rhododendron and blue jay
Their several spots of quiet gladness keep
For the sad eye, while o'er the wooded steep
The heavy bee drones on all drowsily,
Storing, while it may, its treasures sweet.

And, as the soul of some fair Quakeress
In silent message listening for the stress
Of harmonies divine, finds life instead,
And humbly shrinking at the thought,
Drops her impassioned eye full guiltily,
Hangs down in shame her head,
So I delighted in this quiet place,
Felt ideal peace and restfulness efface
All worldy thought, and reverent as a child
Joyed in dear nature's benediction mild.

The oak tree sought the void
Believing mind, given an aim
Messaged to stalwart root
The challenge past . . . to trunk, bark, trembly leaf
Winds tortured, toss't and rent
The oak withstood its cleansing,
Then the sun suffered its aspiration,
It too was on its way.

Within a lunar window arching sky and ocean
The Master's dream for slow humanity
Sets forth man's spirit walking on the sea.
"Fear not, Oh little children, come to me,"
The solemn organ tones resound from aisle to nave.
Aspiring arches echo the refrain
And humble hearts re-echo it again,
While on the air sweet women's voices rise
In praise and trust. They are not wise.
They can but trust and pray and labor
For their loved ones, ignorantly perhaps,
Yet silently they listen for the Voice
And make their lives receptive;
Tread the way of pain and sacrifice
And call it Joy and Love.
They ask no more . . . to serve and to rejoice.

Blithe bird, 'twas I once thought to be
A happy voice in this glad world, and gay,
But my sad soul knows too much misery,
I leave my song of gladness unto thee,
This soul to sorrow born,
Joy cannot sing
'Twas born to mourn.
Yes, take thee to the wing,
Thou couldst not understand so grave and
Sad a thing.

THE ROSE

Rose that unfolds beneath the kindly light
Of Godhead, living toward itself unseen,
One germ of earth-life quickened into green,
Urged by what mystic instinct, what blind sight!
Roots know not.
Struggling to express the might of faith,
Denying the dark world between,
Staunch rootlets sought,
And the whole dreary scene
Was changed to leaf and flower
And perfume exquisite.
And yet the roots are of the rose a part
And the sweet perfume dies with the frail flower.
But do you think that the great cosmic heart
Does not include the dark, aspiring hour,
Nor cherish all the rose's little dower?

As the years roll on and life's cares heap up higher
My soul tries forever to smother its sighing
For the free life in forest and meadow, when I sang
With the birds for the joy of the sunrise, and felt
On my brow the cool gems that the night fays
Lost from their hair when in midst of their revels
They fled 'fore the Sun God's shield to the eastward,
The flaming disk that he carries before him
Driving the stars and the moon and the darkness
Back from the heavens, that crops may flourish
And quickening health brown man's cheek
And cheer his heart up, making life grateful
After the pale, still rest of the night time.

O for the calm joy in forest and meadow,
The night fay's caress on my life-fevered brow.
Peace of my childhood descend on my spirit,
Strengthen me now.

PAINTINGS

THE GAY NINETIES

AT THE FEET OF THE MASTER

YOUTH EMBARKING ON THE BOAT OF LIFE

END OF THE ROAD, SEA ISLAND, GEORGIA

OPPOSITE PAGE:
EARLY STUDY
PAINTED IN CECILIA BEAUX' STUDIO
AT THE PENNSYLVANIA ACADEMY OF FINE ARTS

ANNE HEEBNER ON THE PORCH AT BOOTHBAY HARBOR

HIGH BUTTON BOOTS

BALLOON WOMAN, PARIS

MARKET WOMAN, GUERNSEY, CHANNEL ISLANDS

TAOS, NEW MEXICO

LOCK, NEW HOPE, PENNSYLVANIA

TAOS, NEW MEXICO